the Running Indians

Previous Book

Dick Lutz (Richard L. Lutz, MSW) is the author of
FEEL BETTER! LIVE LONGER! RELAX. Salem,
Oregon: DIMI PRESS, 1988.

the
RUNNING
INDIANS
The Tarahumara of Mexico

by Dick and Mary Lutz

Dimi Press
Salem, Oregon

DIMI PRESS
3820 Oak Hollow Lane, SE
Salem, Oregon - 97302
Printed in the United States of America
First Edition

Library of Congress Cataloging in Publication

       Data:

Lutz, Richard L., 1929-
    The running Indians : the Tarahumara of
    Mexico / by Dick and Mary Lutz. — 1st ed.
      p.   cm.
    Bibliography: p.
    Includes index.
    ISBN: 0-931625-19-x : (pbk.)
    1. Tarahumara Indians. I. Lutz, Mary. II. Title
F1221.T25L88 1989
972' . 00497—dc19   88-23765

                             CIP

To our parents, Charles and Mabel Lutz and Peter and Gertrude Koreman, who taught us to live life with the intellectual curiosity that brought about this book.

TABLE OF CONTENTS

ILLUSTRATIONS

FOREWORD

We runners make the mistake of looking at the Tarahumara Indians the way we used to view people who ran marathons. When U.S. marathoners were so few they could all fit into a high school gym, runners who didn't run that far thought anyone who did was a visitor from another planet. We couldn't think of ourselves doing what they did. This mistaken thinking took a while to correct itself. But now we know that almost anyone can run a marathon— maybe not a fast one, but a full one.

Many writers have described the Tarahumaras and their incredible running abilities. These Indians from Mexico routinely run distances covered only by the most advanced ultra-marathoners from north of the border. Legend has it that a marathon promoter once invited a team of Tarahumaras to his race. When the Indians learned how short the distance was, they sent only women.

The mistake writers made up to now was holding the Tarahumaras in too much awe. They were pictured as noble savages whose feats had nothing to do with what we runners do. After all, these Indians grew up with running as their only way to travel, carry messages or go for food. How could a modern runner make up for that lifetime of conditioning?

Maybe we can't close the gap entirely. But the Tarahumara story should give evidence that whatever one group of humans can do, all humans have the potential to do. If these disease-prone, undernourished Indians can run all day in the mountains in sandals, we healthy, well-fed, well-shod runners can develop similar abilities.

Dr. George Sheehan writes in <u>This Running Life</u>, "Have the Tarahumaras received a special dispensation from some of the human limitations known to us? If they have, I suspect it is because these limitations are artificial. They have been based on our imperfect knowledge of what man can and cannot do."

The Tarahumaras show us what we once were; we all came from stock which crossed continents on foot. They show us, too, what we might again become as runners; the ability to go all day hasn't been bred out of us.

Dick and Mary Lutz tell their story in text and photos. Read it not as an example of the impossible but as a lesson in how we all might be able to run if conditions were different.

Joe Henderson
Authority on running

ACKNOWLEDGEMENTS

The help of many people was utilized in the preparation of this book. The bibliography cites the written work which we have built upon. This book would not have been nearly so adequate without references to these authors. Also, we thank the many librarians who helped us obtain research material, particularly those of the Pueblo Regional Library in Pueblo, Colorado; the Umatilla County Library in Pendleton, Oregon; and the Salem City Library (especially Conrad Pfeiffer) and the Oregon State Library in Salem, Oregon. Editorial assistance was provided by Linda Bowers, Lenny Erickson, and Judy Lutz. Eileen Mooso performed the arduous task of typing the manuscript into a computer. Doug DuBosque designed the cover. Judy Lutz did the final and definitive work on the manuscript. Several people have read the manuscript in various stages of development and provided many helpful comments. These include our children Jim, Judy, Anita, Sherry, and David Lutz. Special thanks go to Roberto Valenzuela, our Mexican guide, and to Marcos Garcia, our Tarahumara friend. We owe a deep debt of gratitude to all who made this book possible.

PREFACE

While living in Pueblo, Colorado and vacationing periodically in Mexico, we determined to explore the Barranca del Cobre and learn what we could about the fascinating Tarahumara Indians. The Tarahumara have intrigued us for years and we have done considerable research concerning them.

Our research has included two trips into their vast country. On one of these trips we hiked to the bottom of a deep canyon. The trips were primarily photographic expeditions. The Tarahumara are such shy and reserved people that it is impossible to get to know them and to understand their lifestyle in a short visit. Several scientists have spent months among them and some of these are quoted in the text.

The book took years to write and publish so perhaps some of the specific references are somewhat dated. We do not feel that has materially changed our account and the perspective of time has probably improved some of our conclusions.

Traveling in rural Mexico is adventuresome, but not impossibly primitive. We camped out three nights and certainly met many friendly, helpful people. Dick is a Clinical Social Worker and Mary a

Registered Nurse. We do not consider ourselves 'fitness freaks'. Although we have done some hiking we really were not in very good physical shape. Dick had had knee surgery some six months before our hike into the canyon and experienced no problems as a result. The hike from El Divisadero to the Rio Urique took us nine hours and was hard by our standards.

Contrast this with M. John Fayhee in his article in BACKPACKER magazine in November, 1987. He describes the identical journey as taking "six pleasant hours". It was much easier than another hike he made in the area. We guess that the difficulty of a hike depends not only upon such variables as age and condition but also upon previous hiking experiences. In traveling we made no reservations and experienced no difficulty as a result.

If this book whets the reader's appetite for learning more about the Tarahumara and results in his or her going to the Barrancas, we will have fulfilled our goal.

Dick and Mary Lutz
Salem, Oregon

INTRODUCTION

In writing this book we have organized it into four parts. We use the term parts, rather than chapters, to emphasize the very different focus of each section. The four parts describe the four aspects of the Tarahumara which we found most fascinating.

The Tarahumara Indians live in isolated clusters throughout an extremely rugged area of northwestern Mexico. Probably the most outstanding feature of the Tarahumara is their incredible ability at long-distance running. As a group, the Tarahumara are the greatest endurance runners in the world. The Tarahumara runners do not formally train. They smoke cigarettes, get drunk every few weeks, and eat very little, yet they can run for days and nights at a time. Seeking to answer the questions "why?" and "how?" is one of the primary issues addressed in Part I.

Part II consists of a discussion of the fascinating Tarahumara culture. People who have heard of the Tarahumara usually are familiar only with their endurance running. The Tarahumara culture is extremely interesting in itself and particularly unusual is its durability. The Tarahumara are considered part of the Uto-Aztecan linguistic group and are related to the Apaches of the southwestern United States. It is believed that the Tarahumara were once cannibalistic, but they are certainly a gentle, non-violent people today. The individual Tarahumara tends to withdraw from any form of conflict or argument. He is sensitive, proud, and shy. The Tarahumara share their huge territory with many Mexicans, but are distinctive in their language, dress, and social customs. The Mexican government is protective of the Indians and has set up a Supreme Council of the Tarahumara.

The rugged and beautiful terrain in which the Tarahumara live is described in Part III. This is the aspect which can most easily be pictured and we hope that the photographs we have included convey the feeling of the Barranca del Cobre. For a photographer the Barranca del Cobre is a paradise of beautiful views, interesting plant life, and startling scenes. For those adventurous types who are in good condition, we heartily recommend a hike into this beautiful canyon.

The concluding Part IV describes a facet of the Tarahumara tribe which is also striking. That is their geographic location and the ease of visiting them. We have estimated that approximately seventy million people (forty million Mexicans and thirty million Americans) live within 1000 air miles of Creel, the bustling town which is in the heart of the Tarahumara country and is its largest population center. With access provided by the spectacular railroad (less than thirty years old) it is surprisingly convenient to visit the Barranca del Cobre as well as other sections of the Sierra Madre which are inhabited by the Tarahumara. We have intentionally avoided details of schedules and prices because these change so frequently. For example, the Mexican peso was devalued between our first and second trips to the Barranca del Cobre. A handmade violin that sold for $8 (U.S. money) on the first trip cost us only $5 on the second.

A word of explanation is in order concerning the names of the areas discussed in this book. The mountain range encompassing the territory occupied by the Tarahumara is known as the Sierra Madre Occidental (Mother Mountain Range of the West). The more specific area which is considered the land of the Tarahumara is called the Barranca del Cobre (Copper Canyon) or, occasionally, the Sierra Tarahumara. Confusingly, the Barranca del Cobre is also the name of a specific canyon which has the Rio Urique at its bottom.

PART I

THE RUNNING INDIANS

"The Tarahumara may be the finest natural distance runners in the world."

> Michael Jenkinson
> WILD RIVERS OF NORTH
> AMERICA, 1973

"Probably not since the days of the ancient Spartans has a people achieved such a high state of physical conditioning."

> Dale Groom, M.D.
> American Heart Journal,
> 1971

The Tarahumara are amazing endurance runners. They may run 200 miles over a period of three days and nights. To this day, one of the methods used by the Tarahumara to hunt deer is to chase the animal until it drops from exhaustion. Rabbits and wild turkeys are also hunted in this manner. Within recent decades the Tarahumara were sometimes hired by nearby ranchers to chase and capture wild horses.

Two Tarahumara were entered in the 1928 Olympics in Amsterdam. They competed in the marathon (about twenty six and a half miles) and lost. When it was explained to them that the race was over, they exclaimed "Too short! Too short!" Evidently they were prepared to run much further and were, in effect, just getting warmed up.

These remarkable Indians run races in a unique fashion that is as much a game as a race. The kickball race, rarajipari, may be the most striking feature of the Tarahumara culture. A rarajipari generates a great deal of enthusiasm among the Indians and considerable betting takes place. The stakes may be livestock, personal possessions, or money. The bets may be substantial, with the winning racers receiving a small share of the proceeds. In the rarajipari two teams of three to ten men compete. Each team has a ball, about the size of a baseball, which has been carved from wood. One of the team members flips the ball forward with his foot along the designated course. Team members take turns in advancing the ball by this method. The object of the race is to be the first team to get its ball over the finish line. Pennington, in his 1963 book, THE TARAHUMAR OF MEXICO, describes the setting:

> The race course ... is commonly laid out upon a circuit that is clearly defined by stones, notches in trees, or in some instances marked by men who stand and act as points, about which the runners turn. Invariably, the course is laid out at an elevation below the spectators, who prefer to sit or stand upon high ground and watch, while shouting encouragement to their favorites. The circuit may be long or short, and the number of turns around the course usually depends upon the distance covered. The race may last a few minutes, a day, or several days; the runners may take time out for rest

and refreshment in the longer races.

The rarajipari is normally a contest between two teams from neighboring settlements. Each team has one or more medicine men who function somewhat like the team's coach, chaplain and trainer. The medicine man (or shaman) performs various procedures to help his team win. He massages the runners legs with special ointments. He also performs certain rituals for the purpose of protecting his runners from the magic of the opposing team. Different practices are used to disrupt the running of the opposing team members. One of the most curious of these procedures involves the shinbone of an old skeleton which has been retrieved from a Tarahumara burial cave. The bone is ground up into a powder and the powder buried on the course. The Tarahumara believe that the spirit of the dead person will rise up and grab the legs of those running over the spot, thus slowing them down. The team whose shaman placed the powder is warned to avoid the spot.

Another ritual the team may go through takes place the night before the race. After the team ball for the rarajipari has been carved, the team shaman takes it to a burial cave. A leg bone is dug up and the ball, the bone, bowls of food, and a jar of tesguino (the native drink) are placed before a cross. Next, the shaman asks the spirit of the dead person to weaken his team's opponents.

Sometimes, the ritual the night before the race consists of the runners and the shaman burning candles which have been placed on either side of a small wooden cross. The shaman chants and sings while the runners circle around the cross and candles. The runners circle the same number of times as the laps in the next day's rarajipari.

During the preparations on the day of the race, certain herbs are scattered in the wind to poison opposing runners. Each magical "attack" has its antidote or "defense" used by the opposing side.

Cheating is not uncommon during a race, but one method of counteracting it is for runners to smoke a mixture of dried turtle blood, dried bat blood, and tobacco. Runners do not refrain from smoking tobacco prior to a race, although they do refrain from drinking tesguino or eating fat, eggs, potatoes, or sweets. Also, they avoid contact with women for several days before a race.

Taking the various actions based on superstitious beliefs is apparently effective. The main reason why teams sometimes drop out of a <u>rarajipari</u> is superstition, not exhaustion.

The <u>rarajipari</u> runners carry fetishes in the race to make themselves strong and rattles to keep themselves awake. These may be hawk heads, vulture heads, glowworms, or rattles made of deer-hooves and bamboo.

Before the start of the race, an official gives final instructions which may include the reminder that any runner who picks up the ball and throws it will be disqualified. He will also wind up in hell!

The <u>rarajipari</u> is a major social event for the Tarahumara. Scores of spectators frequently run along with the runners early in the race, encouraging their favorites and discouraging the opposition. A favorite ploy used against the other team is to ask the runner what his wife is up to while he is racing. A great deal of fun accompanies the <u>rarajipari</u>. Perhaps there should be something like the <u>rarajipari</u> in American long distance running.

Women also are runners but they have their

own racing game. It is called <u>dowerami</u>. Instead of a ball, the women use a pair of interlocking hoops, made of bear grass, which they advance by throwing with a curved stick. Betting also goes on for the women's races. The distances are long, but not as long as for some of the men's races.

One of the most impressive reports in the literature of races is the account of two Tarahumara sisters running twenty eight and a half miles in slightly less than five hours. This is not fantastic speed when compared, for example, to the Boston Marathon, but it is remarkable for a couple of un-trained teenage girls in long dresses running over a rough terrain at a high altitude. Women sometimes run with their babies in shawls on their backs.

Probably the longest run (not race) on record is that of a Tarahumara man running nearly 600 miles in five days to deliver an important message.

The Tarahumara do not run at a fast pace. The outstanding aspect of their racing ability is endur-ance, not speed. An authority on Mexican sport has stated of the Tarahumara, "There is no doubt they are the best runners in the world, not for speed but for distance." The Tarahumara do not do well in formal races like the Olympics because of the strangeness of their surroundings. The runners, before the race, are served food that they are not used to. The track is flat and at least part of it is around an oval. The Tarahumara do not like to run on flat ground because they find it difficult to judge distances there. In the Olympics, the Tarahumara are expected to wear running shoes rather than the simple sandals they prefer. It is not surprising that the Tarahumara are reluctant to participate in races away from their homeland.

The explanation of the remarkable endurance of the Tarahumara has been sought by several scientists. One team of physiologists studied the reactions of the participants in a race. Pulse rate, blood pressure, serum cholesterol, hemoglobin, and hematocrit were all measured. Careful records were kept of velocity (distance divided by time), and elevation of the race area and the weight, height, and age of the runners. From these factors, the energy expenditure was estimated and Balke and Snow drew this conclusion in their 1965 paper in the American Journal of Physical Anthropology, "The average performance during the nearly seven hour effort exceeded the maximum work capacity of the 'normal' American male who can maintain the same pace for only about fifteen minutes." These studies included Tarahumara youngsters who had lived for some years at a mission school and thus had become accustomed to running much less than their more primitive peers. The mission children did not do nearly as well on their running tests. This observation led the scientists to the tentative conclusion that Tarahumara endurance is more a matter of conditioning than heredity.

Dale Groom, an Oklahoma physician, also did examinations before, during, and after a rarajipari. His detailed article in the American Heart Journal in 1971 will be of interest to physicians. This article reproduces both electrocardiograms and chest x-rays of Tarahumara runners. Groom comments, "Almost unbelievable is the pulmonary performance of these runners who, after running competitively for hours, cross the finish line and stand quietly without panting while one examines them, seemingly unperturbed by the effort." Of course, it should be remembered that Dr. Groom was examining the runners after a 'short' race of only some twenty eight miles through extremely rugged terrain seven to eight thousand feet above sea level. Dr. Groom found that neither heart capacity nor respiratory capacity are limiting factors in Tarahumara endurance running.

Leg pain does occur in Tarahumara runners, but it is usually muscular rather than joint pain. Questioning of Tarahumara runners has not turned up a single recollection of a runner dropping out of a race due to chest pain or shortness of breath. Apparently, changes in frequency of urination do occur and cause concern among some of the runners. Groom summarizes, "Several of the more dramatic 'end points' of physical exertion described in the literature did not seem to hold for the Tarahumara."

The "athletes heart", referring to an enlarged organ, is mentioned occasionally in medical literature. If anyone were a candidate for this condition, it would seem to be the Tarahumara runner, but there is no evidence that the situation exists in the Indians. One of the physiological mysteries that remain is how the bodies of the Tarahumara runners cope with large oxygen debts while they are running a mile and a half above sea level. Groom thinks that one clue to the solution may lie in the decrease rather than increase in blood pressure during and immediately after running. Several groups of scientists have found pulse rates and blood pressure to be about 20% below normal.

An interesting study was reported in the

medical journal, PSYCHOPHYSIOLOGY, (March, 1981). Male Tarahumaras were compared to American male marathon runners and long distance bicyclists living in Boulder, Colorado (which is at a similar altitude to the Barranca del Cobre). Subjects were matched for age and tested for heart rate, systolic and diastolic blood pressure, and mean arterial pressure. All the men were tested at rest, at peak exercise, and one minute past exercise. All blood pressures were lower in the Indians by a significant (but not huge) amount. Other differences were not statistically significant. As with most research, the report of this study ends with the comment that more research needs to be done.

A major factor in the Tarahumara's amazing endurance running seems to be their diet, which is almost meatless, and the quantity of their food intake, which is much less than the average American's. Nathan Pritikin, who developed the Pritikin Diet, states that the diet of the Tarahumara contains about 10% protein, 10% fat, and 80% complex carbohydrates. This is roughly equivalent to his Diet.

James Fixx, in his bestselling book on running, refers to the almost unbelievable feats of endurance running performed by the Tarahumara and

states that their diet is very similar to the one advo-
cated by our own vegetarians.

However, Groom contends, "diet is hardly a
plausible explanation" for the Tarahumara's incredible endurance running.

Careful review of a number of scientific studies results in the conclusion that there are two main
causative factors to the phenomenal endurance of
the Tarahumara runner: 1) physical conditioning
and 2) the cultural importance of running.

Physical conditioning occurs as a result of the
great amount of running the Tarahumara do over
the rugged terrain of the Sierra Madre Occidental.
The habit begins in childhood. The Indians run
almost everywhere they go, apparently because they
like to. Also, foot travel is very practical in the
Tarahumara country. The Sierra Madre has few
roads and many paths, with some of the paths being
easier to negotiate on foot than by burro or mule. The
Indians are faster than animals and go further in a
day. They frequently carry heavy objects such as
railroad ties and mining timbers up or down the
steep mountain slopes. This continuous foot travel

over an incredibly rugged land results in nearly every Tarahumara being in superb physical condition. Many Tarahumara families move with the seasons and their small plots of land are frequently miles from where the family lives. Every member of the family must be able to travel for long distances in order to perform his everyday tasks. Materially, the Tarahumara own little, but what they have must be carried when they move.

The cultural importance of running is a more subtle component of the Tarahumara endurance. A significant fact is that the Tarahumara call themselves raramuri which means "fleet foot" or "foot runner." Evidently, the Tarahumara have historically identified themselves as outstanding runners. As Groom says, "Being fleet of foot is at the same time his livelihood, his recreation, and his criterion of success." Among the Tarahumara, it is important to be a good runner. Also, a special popularity with women is said to be an incentive to win at rarajipari.

An attempt has been made in this chapter to summarize and interpret the scientific thinking about what makes the Tarahumara the greatest long distance runners in the world. It is obvious that much

of what is written (both here and elsewhere) is
speculation based on inadequate factual knowledge.
For example, the primitiveness of the physiological
tests is repeatedly commented upon by the testers.
They had to use portable equipment and the physical environment was not conducive to sophisticated
testing. The superstitious beliefs of the Tarahumara
made certain procedures impossible. The shyness of
the women was a determining (and negative) factor
on at least one occasion. A team of scientists per-
suaded the Tarahumara to set up a women's race as
well as a race for men. The women raced, but
absolutely refused to be examined or even inter-
viewed afterward.

The rest of the world has much to learn from
the Tarahumara, including not only the reasons they
are able to perform such feats of endurance running,
but also the beautiful aspects of their culture.

PART II

THE TARAHUMARA CULTURE

"These Indians form one of the largest tribes of North American aborigines, and they remain at present one of the most isolated and primitive Indian groups on our continent and one of the few semi-nomadic cave-dwelling races in the world."

> D. Carleton Gadjusek
> The Geographical Review,
> 1953

"The most striking thing about the Tarahumara since the turn of the century is the almost complete absence of change in their culture."

> J.R. Champion
> Transactions of the NY
> Academy of Sciences, 1955

With the possible exception of their isolation, these statements are as true in the '80s as when they were written in the '50s.

There are about 50,000 Tarahumara Indians scattered throughout a large area of northwestern Mexico. The most interesting subgroup of the Tarahumara live in the wilds of the Barranca del Cobre (Copper Canyon) and other nearby canyons. For at least part of the year, many of the canyon dwellers live in caves. Most canyon dwellers move up and down the canyons with the change in seasons. Although they move to new locations seasonally, they still raise crops. The fact that they live in a wild and rugged area of Mexico results in their having been studied and visited by many fewer people than their proximity to the United States would suggest.

This very difficulty of access has helped to lessen the inroads of civilization and permits the continued existence near the United States of a basically Stone Age culture. It is a great deal easier to visit the Barranca del Cobre than New Guinea or Africa to see much the same things.

The Tarahumara have been in the same area with an essentially unchanged style of living for centuries. Their first recorded contact with outsiders was in 1607 when a Jesuit priest named Juan Fonte intervened in a conflict between two Indian groups, the Tarahumaras and the Tepehuanes. Fonte was, after nine years, killed by the Tepehuanes, but the missionaries had come. The first Tarahumara mission was established in 1639 by Jose Pascual, a Jesuit priest. From 1767 to 1900, the missionaries were priests of the Franciscan order rather than Jesuits. Perhaps the peaceloving nature of the Franciscans had some effect on the Tarahumara culture. This theory is questionable in view of Merrill's statement that, "The priests are peripheral to the Indians' religious life, performing baptisms and an occasional mass but little else, and few actually live in Tarahumara communities". The priests also operate schools and hospitals for them.

In 1648 the Tarahumara rebelled for the first time against the Spanish, particularly those exploiting the Tarahumara in the gold mines. Warfare and horrible atrocities continued sporadically until 1698. It was probably after this period that the Tarahumara began their attitudes of passive resistance, withdrawal, and avoidance. These characteristics of the Tarahumara continue today.

The discovery of silver near what is now the city of Chihuahua in 1709 resulted in a renewed period of exploitation of the Indians by the Spanish. This time the Tarahumara did not go to war and many of them gave up and merged into the general population of Mexico. Others, however, maintained their cultural integrity, although the extent of the Tarahumara territory declined. Perhaps this drawing away from the dominant culture has aided in the remarkable stability shown by the Tarahumara culture over the years. From 1800 to 1825 Apache attacks were widespread and years later, in 1917, Pancho Villa's raiders spread disorder and disease in the region.

The Tarahumara are a very reserved people. This has contributed to their not having been extensively studied. We heard of one American who camped in the Barranca del Cobre for five months with hopes of getting to know the Indians. He was unable to talk to even one of them, although a family did give him some leather to repair his shoe when it wore out. The Tarahumara people are not hostile, however, but simply reserved and shy.

Our first encounter with this reserve occurred on our visit to a village named Samachic. The

Mexican government has provided a small store for the Indians who are the population of this village. After stepping into this store, we went outside to where two men were sitting on a wooden bench. We asked one of the men for permission to take his picture. Not only would the man not speak, he would not even look up! The Indian then rose and walked away while the other fellow (obviously bold for a Tarahumara) looked up, nodded, stood up, and allowed his picture to be taken. The youth received not only a peso from us, but taunting remarks from some young men watching from the porch of a nearby school. Apparently, he was far too friendly to suit his peers and he quickly walked off with his head down.

The children, though, are not this shy. Although far from bold, they are as curious as most children are. On our hikes in the canyon we frequently passed caves occupied by families. The children would emerge from the family cave to watch us. Sometimes when we returned along the same route, the women were standing in front of their caves with handmade articles to sell. They said nothing but simply held their crude goods so we could see them. When asked the price, they shyly told us and then delivered their handmade goods in return for the few coins requested. Although the actions of these women are passive by American or Mexican standards, they are active, even assertive, by Tarahumara standards.

During these brief transactions in front of the family's cave, the men of the family were peering out from behind the rock wall that constitutes the front of their home. This shyness extends to close family members as well. Husband and wife rarely look at each other while talking. One of the few evidences of affection between spouses that has been observed is the women combing their husband's hair. This extreme shyness, even between close family members, is a characteristic of the Tarahumara culture. The bashfulness breaks down only at the social events which are known as <u>tesguinadas</u>.

One of the most important aspects of the life of a Tarahumara is his/her isolation. The individual Tarahumara lives and works alone, although family ties result in a limited amount of interaction. The soil is poor, much of it is too steep to be tillable, and there are no large fields. Kennedy, in his 1978 book, THE TARAHUMARA OF THE SIERRA MADRE, reports his calculations that in one part of the Tarahumara range, the average amount of cultivated land per person is about one fourth of an acre. A family will grow its crops in several different plots, perhaps miles apart. This contributes to the isolation. The individuals, except young children, go about their own tasks during the day (such as herding, working in the fields, or cooking) and are usually alone. Sometimes, the individual Tarahumara does absolutely nothing for a period of hours. Families come together at night, but exhaustion, custom, and the lack of light make for an early bedtime.

The usual housing pattern (outside of permanent villages) is a scattered grouping of families. Since the families are mobile and they move to different areas, neighborhood groupings change with the seasons. The Tarahumara thus has seasonal neighbors.

The tesguinada is a very valuable antidote to all this isolation. It is an extremely important part of the Tarahumara culture. Kennedy calls the tesguinada "a psychological and social response to the isolation imposed by the mode of life in the rugged Sierra Madre." A tesguinada can be compared to the traditional American barnraising, as it is an occasion when neighbors get together at the home of a family for the purpose of working together on a project for the benefit of that family. The project may be the building of a new fence for the goat corral, the building of a new dwelling, or the weeding of a plot of land. After the project is completed (or sometimes before completion), the host family serves food and drink to all hands. The Tarahumara make a beer from corn sprouts which is prepared especially for this party. The beer, tesguino, is the most important part of the tesguinada.

Tesguino spoils rapidly and thus only enough is made for one specific tesguinada and all that is made is consumed there. The drink has a relatively low alcoholic content and a high expense (in corn). Evidently, the Tarahumara have a high tolerance for alcohol. The drinking of tesguino is more a social than an individual activity.

At the tesguinada, the corn beer is drunk by both men and women in a somewhat ritualistic fashion for the purpose of getting as inebriated as possible. Drunkenness is a matter of pride, not of shame. The Tarahumara speak of a "beautiful intoxication." Shining eyes, laughing, and singing are aspects of behavior that appear almost only at tesguinadas. Also, flirting, lovemaking, and fighting occur. Both male and female reserve breaks down, and the woman is as likely to be the pursuer as the pursued.

It has been said that virtually all human beings carry within themselves a latent hostility and a desire to violate the sexual mores of their culture. The Tarahumara have found a place to vent these feelings in a way that is seldom harmful and does not disrupt the society. The Tarahumara mechanism is the tesguinada. Nothing short of murder is definitely prohibited. Although fighting and adultery are preached against at the start of every tesguinada, they almost always happen and are almost always blamed on the tesguino and forgotten. Probably 90% or more of all social infractions which occur among the Tarahumara take place at tesguinadas. Perhaps the traditional gentleness of the Tarahumara people is possible because the frequent tesguinadas enable them to release their violent emotions in a relatively safe manner at a designated time and place.

Lumholtz, in his classic work on the Sierra Madre area, UNKNOWN MEXICO (1902), has stated that were it not for tesguino, the Tarahumara would not be able to reproduce (because of their shyness). Kennedy estimates that the average Tarahumara spends upwards of 100 days a year at tesguinadas or recovering from their effects. Additionally, the corn that must be diverted into the making of tesguino helps to keep the family impoverished. Given the poverty of the land and its people, the tesguinada would seem to be a wasteful practice. But given the isolation and shyness of the people, the ritual can only be seen as an advantageous custom both psychologically and culturally. Legend says that tesguino was given to the Tarahumara by God so that they could get their work done and enjoy themselves. The sacred nature of tesguino is shown in many ways, including the fact that a tesguinada is held after every religious fiesta. As Kennedy says, "the meaning and importance of tesguino interpenetrate all major sectors of the culture and social organization."

As we were hiking down into the canyon toward the Rio Urique, we heard the sounds of drums echoing ominously through the canyon. We asked Roberto, our guide, if the Indians were warning each other of our approach and he replied that a family was simply calling their neighbors to a tesguinada. Invitations to tesguinadas are made only when the tesguino is ready.

Some writers have stressed the extreme poverty, malnutrition, and disease of the Tarahumara. Although we saw indications of all three, we were more impressed by the positive aspects of the Tarahumara culture. These Indians are a proud people who obviously do not see themselves as being miserable. As we were talking with Marcos Garcia, our Tarahumara friend, we asked him a question about his ancestry. He replied proudly, "Yo soy Tarahumara!" (I am a Tarahumara!) His expression reflected centuries of pride in his people. Although we took many photographs in the Barranca country, our failure to capture this expression on film remains our biggest disappointment.

The religion of most Tarahumara is Christian, but, as in many tribes, the ancient ways play a major part in their version of Christianity. The religious education of the Indians cannot be said to be sophisticated. For instance, although crude churches exist in many of the villages, there are annual ceremonies for "purifying" them. The ceremonies themselves are essentially pagan.

Although the Mexican priests may say a mass at these ceremonies, the Tarahumara have maintained control of their religion. They consider God their father and they link Him with the sun. God's wife is associated with the moon and is also the Virgin Mary. God's elder brother is the Devil and is the father of all non-Indians. The Tarahumara are more concerned with the present than with the after-life. They feel that to keep things like the weather satisfactory it is necessary to keep both God and the Devil happy.

An example of the way in which Christian doctrine has been distorted is found in Merrill's account of the Tarahumara's view of the significance of the palm leaves distributed by the priest on Palm Sunday. The palm leaves can be burned to prevent hail or boiled to produce a solution that, when drunk, will cure chest pains. The Tarahumara say that the palm's special qualities are due to an event that occurred in the distant past. To again quote Merrill:

"God, God's wife, and the Devil had been drinking maize beer for several hours when God fell asleep and the Devil succeeded in seducing God's wife, largely through his accomplished guitar play-ing. God awoke, catching them *in flagrante delicto* , and a fight ensued. The Devil pulled a knife and God fled, with the Devil in close pursuit. God would surely have been slain had a palm not offered its thick leaves as a hiding place."

We wonder how the Jesuit priests in the Barranca del Cobre feel about this Palm Sunday story.

Long before the Jesuits came, the cross was used as a symbol by the Tarahumara. To them it represents the Tree of Life. Many folk beliefs intertwine the Tarahumara culture and religion. The Indian and Christian beliefs are so blended and blurred together that it is impossible to lift out original Tarahumara religious beliefs.

Robert M. Zingg, in an interesting article in the anthology COYOTE WISDOM (1938), comments about the Tarahumara way of celebrating Christmas by saying that they do it "in abysmal ignorance and grievous error." He also summarizes, "what they lack in knowledge of Christian customs, however, they make up for both in the fervor of their religious feeling and in the jollity and drunken merriment that follow the sacred ceremonies."

One small group of the Tarahumara have never adopted Christianity. These people do not celebrate the many religious events (Christmas, Easter, etc.) as do the majority of the Tarahumara.

The narcotic plant peyote has been used and

probably still is used occasionally by a few, but it is not very important. When taken, peyote may be a part of a ceremonial ritual conducted by a shaman, or it may be taken as a stimulant by a <u>rarajipari</u> runner.

Those Indians who live in the canyons follow a semi-nomadic life, changing elevation with the seasons. Although most of the nomadic families move down into a canyon for the winter for warmth, some move even higher for the purpose of being nearer to a good wood supply.

Many of their dwellings are in caves or under overhanging rock. "Rock shelters" is probably a more accurate term than "caves" for the dwellings many of the Tarahumara occupy. Tarahumara houses usually do not have windows. The houses may partially consist of leaning logs or boards.

The individual household is essentially self-sufficient, with little more in manufactured goods than ax and hoe heads, needles, knives, and cloth. There was no furniture in the cave dwellings or houses we saw. One of the houses seemed better constructed than the others. Although built against a wall of rock, it had three walls of small rocks with a type of mortar between them. It also had a walled, but roofless, patio. We noticed that the wall at the end of the patio had no mortar between the rocks. When we asked why this was, we were told that it was so the family could look through the wall down the trail and see who was coming. In this case the wall serves as a window.

Zingg writes of the annual washing of the clothes by the Tarahumara. We doubt that the washing of clothes still takes place only yearly, but no one could criticize the Tarahumara for excessive cleanliness.

Childbirth involves the Tarahumara woman going alone to a secluded area, preparing a bed of grass, using a tree limb as support, and delivering from a crouched position. Child rearing appears casual and easy (like almost everything in the Tarahumara culture), with breast feeding extending for as long as three years. With no beds in the Tarahumara household, an infant sleeps in its mother's arms at night. After two months, it is carried everywhere on its mother's back in her shawl. Bowel and bladder training is informal and not a source of tension. The Tarahumara have no privies or toilets and use no toilet paper.

Children, like adults, have no regular sleeping habits and simply stay up until they fall asleep. They do their share of the family's work as they grow and do not generally have toys or spend time playing (except for some imitating of adult tasks). Children do not attend <u>tesguinadas</u>. Infant mortality is high, if ten or eleven offspring are born, a family may raise two or three to maturity. Life expectancy is estimated at about age forty-five.

Burial of the dead was formerly done in caves but it is now usually done in cemeteries. To the Tarahumara, death is simply a fact of life - not an end, but a change. Despite this view, it is believed that the spirit of the dead person is capable of doing harm to the living. The correct number (four for women, three for men) of mourning ceremonies is very important so as not to offend the spirit of the dead person. The primary emotion at death rituals is not grief, but fear. This fear seemed to be expressed in a remarkably complete silence at one scene we happened upon.

While driving between Samachic and Creel, we rounded a turn on the gravel road and then slammed on the brakes as we burst into a totally silent crowd of Indians. There must have been about forty of them, with the adults on one side of the road and the children on the other. A truck was in the center of the crowd and something in a green blanket was being lifted onto the bed of the truck. After it was on the truck, the six men who had lifted the object also climbed onto the bed of the truck and took off their hats. It was then that we realized that the object was a dead person. We were still puzzled by the incident and wondered if we had stumbled across a funeral. Later, we learned that a Mexican engineer had been driving along this road, gone off it at the curve, and been killed in the fall down the steep hill. Evidently, what we had come across was a crew of men retrieving the body and a bunch of people silently watching the process. This was in a seemingly sparsely settled area and the mystery of where all these spectators came from remains. It certainly was an eerie scene to stumble on.

The Tarahumara have a language of their own that is related to the languages of a number of other Indian tribes which range from Montana to Central America. The Tarahumara language is spoken in the home, but almost all of the men and some of the women speak Spanish as well.

The Tarahumara do not divide their daily

activities into things done indoors or outdoors. Most activities can take place in either. Eating, in the Tarahumara pattern for nearly everything, follows no routine. People simply eat something when they get hungry (if food is available).

Girls are extremely shy and modest. They are instructed from the age of six or seven never to expose their bodies. As grown women, they do not undress before their husbands. Two of the criteria which men have for feminine beauty are mouse-like eyes and heavy thighs.

The matachine dance, which is the most sophisticated and colorful of the ceremonies held by the Tarahumara, is actually a simplified version of an old Spanish folk dance. Matachine dancing is a relatively recent import and occurs in many Indian tribes that have been influenced by Hispanic culture. The dancers in the matachine are frequently also racers in the rarajipari. One of the reasons for this is the endurance needed to dance for hours.

The Indians make and sell reed baskets, primitive pottery, simple bamboo flutes, handcarved animals and people, and seed necklaces. In addition to these simple items they also make and sell hand carved violins. At first glance, this seems to be an astounding product for a primitive tribe. In the early 1600s the Spaniards moved into the Barranca del Cobre area. The Spaniards taught the Tarahumara how to make violins out of native woods. Today, nearly 400 years later, the Indians are still making violins. The Tarahumara play plaintive and haunting melodies on their stringed instruments. Kennedy reports, "The Tarahumara are literally a society of violinists." The cane flute and drum are ancient Indian instruments which are still used. Guitars are also handmade, but are much less common than violins. Pottery and rough, heavy blankets are made for family use. The blankets are woven by hand from sheep's wool on a crude horizontal loom which is left out in the open.

The usual attire of the Tarahumara male consists of a diaper-like breechcloth, a loose blouse, a plain white headband, and sandals with soles made from old tires. Frequently, this outfit is topped with a Mexican straw hat. The distinctive Tarahumara breechcloth is called a zapeta. It is made from a square piece of cloth folded into a triangle or from two triangular pieces of cloth. The cloth used was formerly woven by hand. One triangle is tied around the waist with the apex brought forward between the legs and up to the belt, the other placed over the first, also tied around the waist but with the triangular apron hanging down behind. Tarahumara women wear much the same types of clothing with the exception of voluminous long skirts instead of the breechcloth. Also, their blouses are likely to be much more colorful. A Tarahumara can identify where another Tarahumara comes from by the details of his dress.

Families raise livestock, especially goats, with the most important function of the animals being to provide fertilizer. The animals are regularly moved from one corral to another when the ground is fertilized enough for growing crops. Because the crops are seasonal, the Tarahumara must store the grain until it is needed. The Tarahumara grain bins are better made than their houses. The reason for this is that if animals get into the grain and eat it, the family may well go hungry.

The Tarahumara diet varies with the season. One of the most common foods is pinole, a fine powder of toasted corn. It is eaten mixed with water. The Tarahumara diet does contain a small amount of meat, particularly goat, which is eaten only on ceremonial occasions. Mice are a delicacy. Just as the

Tarahumara boy grows up doing a lot of running and thus becomes a good runner, he also grows up throwing stones at targets such as birds and squirrels and thus becomes an amazingly accurate thrower, doing much of his hunting in this fashion. Bows and arrows are still made and used as well.

The Tarahumara consider all wild animals potential food with the exception of bears and bats. A bear is thought to have ancestral ties and power and is referred to as "grandfather." There are some 'norteamericanos' who believe that the nearly extinct grizzly bear still exists in the Sierra Madre. Bats are believed to harbor the souls of the dead as they swoop around after dark. It is believed among the Tarahumara that in daylight the souls of the dead sometimes take the form of butterflies. A shaman, by examining the wing markings, can sometimes identify the dead person whose soul is in the butterfly. Another ability of the Tarahumara is being able to follow a bee to its honeycomb.

There are some poisonous snakes in the canyons and, when bitten, the Tarahumara sometimes treat the snake bite victim by holding the snake while the victim bites it back. The cure rate for this technique is not reported. One visiting scientist, Moore,

Natural History, (1951) was offered and ate a dish of ground corn, which had a slimy, yellow appearance. Later he was shown the hairy cases of about 100 black caterpillars, the bodies of which had been used in the dish.

A further addition to the Tarahumara diet is provided by fish stunned by dynamite and then retrieved by diving. Our Tarahumara acquaintance, Marcos, demonstrated this method for us. By prearrangement with our guide, who brought the dynamite, Marcos met us at the Rio Urique deep in the Barranca del Cobre. First, he fashioned for himself a G-string from a native plant. Then, after exploding dynamite in the river, he dove in and retrieved the stunned fish. They did not float to the surface of the water as we expected, but remained several feet under. Marcos looked down for them, either while treading water on the surface or peering from a rock. After locating them, he would dive in and come up with three fish, one in each hand and one in his mouth. The fish were thrown on shore for Roberto to cut open and set out in the sun to dry. The two men each took half of the dried fish home with them. Another method of fishing used by the Tarahumara is to place in the river, upstream from the fish, any of several stupefying drugs extracted from native plants.

Despite this example of cooperation between Mexican and Tarahumara, many of the Indians dislike working for others or for money. They say that money is heavy and will not let them rise to the sky when they die. To the Tarahumara, language and earth are of God, and they cannot sell either. Thus, they are afraid to receive money for teaching their language. The land, also, is a sort of community property that technically belongs to the government. No stranger is allowed to establish himself on the Tarahumara land without permission of the community. Land ownership is a very complicated concept. Individual plots of land are considered to be owned by individual families and are inherited. It is more accurate to say that there are hereditary rights to a particular piece of land. If these rights are not exercised (in other words, if the land is not used) for six years, then the land can be claimed by someone else.

Besides possession of more livestock than most, about the only sign of wealth a rich man shows are his new white <u>zapeta</u> and many strands of beads around the neck of his wife. It is Tarahumara tradition that those who have something another needs should share it when asked. Tarahumara can be seen begging on the streets of the city of Chihuahua and even go door to door in the residential areas. Because of their beliefs, this begging is not demeaning to them. A wealthy Tarahumara is expected to give food to any neighboring family which does not have enough to eat, but this only occurs when the hungry family asks for food.

The completion of the railroad through the Tarahumara country in 1961 has undoubtedly had some effect, but it certainly has not radically changed the cultural patterns. As Kennedy says, the Tarahumara "still retain an independent and viable culture." Missionaries have been in the area since 1607, mining has been carried on since the 17th century, and lumbering since the early 1940s. Each of these developments has had some influence on the culture, but only to a minimal extent. The railroad certainly makes the area more accessible to outsiders.

One of the most outstanding characteristics of the Tarahumara culture is its strength. It has shown itself resistant to change in the past and there is no reason to expect that that characteristic will be any different in the future. In contradistinction to almost every writer who has speculated on the future of the Tarahumara culture, we think it is going to endure. Lumholtz predicted in 1902 that the Tarahumara would disappear in a century. Eighty years later there are probably more of them than there were in Lumholtz's time and their lifestyle is almost identical. As recently as 1979, Fontana declined, in his book TARAHUMARA: WHERE NIGHT IS THE DAY OF THE MOON, to identify specific places for fear that tourists would rush there and spoil it all.

We reject these pessimistic attitudes. The Tarahumara have shown that they are very well able to take care of themselves. If there is one word that describes the Tarahumara, it is endurance, both in their running and in their culture. Kennedy reports that there are signs that the Tarahumara are beginning to resist encroachment on their land and other impositions from the Mexicans.

According to anthropologist Linton in ACCULTURATION IN SEVEN AMERICAN INDIAN TRIBES (1940), "A culture may be defined as the sum total of the knowledge, attitudes and habitual behavior patterns shared and transmitted by the members of a particular society." In examining Tarahumara culture some superficial changes in recent years are observed. Most of the men now wear the typical Mexican straw hat more than the traditional Tarahumara headband. Many of the men work for Mexican employers, particularly in lumbering or mining. During the last years of the building of the railroad, many of the Tarahumara became skilled operators of earthmoving equipment. These, and other developments, do not represent changes in "knowledge, attitudes and habitual behavior patterns." Thus, the superficial changes noted do not really represent culture change. The Tarahumara culture is almost unchanged since Lumholtz.

The single most important reason for the strength of the Tarahumara culture is to be found in the anthropological concept of ethnocentrism. The Unabridged Random House Dictionary defines ethnocentrism as "the belief in the inherent superiority of one's own group and culture accompanied by a feeling of contempt for other groups and cultures." Such a belief is central to the Tarahumara culture, as many of their legends demonstrate. For instance, Burgess in PODRIAS VIVIR COMO UN TARAHU-MARA? states that the Tarahumara consider themselves the most important beings in the world. He recounts a legend of the Tarahumara that says they were created by God, but Mexicans and others were created by the devil. Only God was able to give the devil's creations life and he did, but he did not give them very much life. He blew breath into them twice and three times into the Tarahumara. This is the reason the Tarahumara believe they do not get sick or die as easily as other people. Another legend is that Mexicans do not rise as high up into the sky when they die as do the Tarahumara. Although they have traded with the Mexicans for hundreds of years, the Tarahumara basically do not like most of them. The Running Indians have a vague description of hell, but they do know that the devil has a bitchy wife and all the devil's children are Mexicans.

According to Professor Linton, a culture which considers itself superior to another with which it has contact will not absorb significant elements of the "inferior" culture into its own. It may absorb utilitarian elements (an example is the Tarahumara adopting the Mexican hat, which is very practical, considering the Sierra Madre sun) but it will not quickly assimilate a practice such as a religious ritual. More than any other single thing, we believe that this anthropological concept describes the reason for the striking resistance to change of the Tarahumara culture.

The Tarahumara cultural traits vary at different places in their vast range. A ritual observed at one location may be unheard of a few miles away. For instance, in parts of the Tarahumara range, rarajiparis take place during a tesguinada with the participants drunk. (How many of our endurance races start at cocktail parties?)

The Tarahumara are not a dying race. In fact, their numbers have greatly increased since the coming of the Spanish nearly four centuries ago. With their numbers increasing and their culture resistant to change, the Tarahumara will be around for a long time.

The Tarahumara culture stresses the value of independence. As Kennedy says, "The idea that each individual has a right to determine his own course of action without interference from others is one of the most pervading themes of Tarahumara behavior."

The Tarahumara are an amazing people. Their outstanding ability as long distance runners is their most remarkable characteristic, but not their only interesting one. Their pride and reserve, their shyness, their living in caves, their semi-nomadic way of life, and many other things combine to make the Tarahumara a fascinating people. The rugged beauty of their land is also a part of the attraction of the Tarahumara.

PART III

BARRANCA DEL COBRE

"The Barranca del Cobre is one of the most extensive, isolated, and unexplored canyons systems in the world."

M. John Fayhee
BACKPACKER, 1987

"Seeing the Barranca del Cobre, he called it a 'stupendous gorge'. He descended part of the way and then climbed off his mule, 'sweating and trembling all over from fright. For there opened on the left a chasm the bottom of which could not be seen, and on the right rose perpendicular walls of solid rock'."

Jesuit priest, 1684

The unique Tarahumara live in an equally unique area. The roughness of the countryside defies description. The region has never been thoroughly mapped or even completely explored. There are five main canyons in the Tarahumara country which are probably deeper than the Grand Canyon of Arizona. The Barranca del Cobre is sometimes called Mexico's Grand Canyon. In contrast to its American near-equal, the Barranca del Cobre is extensively covered with vegetation. It receives considerably more rainfall and is thus more hospitable (or less inhospitable) to life. The difference in rainfall also results in the two canyons having a very different beauty. The Barranca del Cobre has a great deal of green among its hues, while the Grand Canyon's walls have more red and orange. The vegetation changes dramatically as one hikes down into the canyon. Most of the trees around the rim are pine or oak, but in the canyon one encounters more tropical cactus, bamboo, banana, and orange trees. Sugar cane grows wild and is also raised as a crop in certain areas. The mountains range to over 9000 feet. The dry season is February through May; the rainy months are July and August; the hottest month is July and the coldest is December. September sees the most flowers.

The climate of the region occupied by the Tarahumara tribe is described as the coldest in Mexico. It is not unheard of for Indians to be found frozen to death along the trail, having passed out while returning from a tesguinada.

The area has seen mining of several minerals, including copper, gold, silver, lead, and zinc, for centuries. Some mining continues to this day. Once in a while, a Tarahumara will bring some gold dust to a Mexican, but he is evasive as to where it comes from. The Tarahumara have good reason to downplay the exploitation of gold and other metals, because their people have suffered and died over the centuries while working the mines for Spaniards and Mexicans. Instead, they bring out calcita (calcite) to sell the traveler.

The hike we made down to the Rio Urique was the best of our hiking career and by far the most difficult. We were farsighted enough to hire a guide with a burro for the trip. Without the guide, we would have become hopelessly lost on the maze of trails. The only American we met in the Barranca del Cobre was a young man who was hiking by himself without a guide. He admitted that he had walked a lot further than necessary because he had been lost so much. The burro, too, was a lifesaver. If we had had to carry our own packs instead of letting Porco do it for us, we surely would not have made it to the bottom of the canyon in nine hours. The length of the trail from Divisadero to the Rio Urique has been estimated at fifteen to eighteen miles.

The trail was incredible in its ruggedness. There were several occasions when Roberto had to lead Porco on a longer path around a section where the burro was simply too wide to get through. For part of the hike, Mary actually walked down the trail backward (like climbing down a ladder) because her knee tendons hurt less this way. Roberto was very impatient with us and obviously thought we were ridiculously slow. When we finally sighted the river on the way down, we thought we were almost there, but it turned out that we spent two more hours on the trail.

In the 1970's the Mexican government constructed a rough footbridge over the Rio Urique deep in the canyon. This was virtually the first sign of "civilization" in the canyon that is known as the Barranca del Cobre.

Along the trail we observed several different

kinds of butterflies, as well as many wasps and bees. We also met several Indians on the trail who invariably smiled shyly as we passed. It was the dry season (February) and we, of course, carried canteens of water. Roberto traveled without a canteen as he several times got water from hidden springs that we would never have found. The spring water was cold and clear. We saw little wildlife on the trail, although it is said that deer still exist.

The goal of our hike down was to reach the Rio Urique. The river was not the dramatic rush of water it becomes at certain times of the year. Flash floods have caused it to rise suddenly more than forty-five feet in the narrower parts of the canyon. If one is camping along the Rio Urique, it should only be in the dry season.

The contrast between cultures was brought home vividly on the nights we camped on the sand at the edge of the Rio Urique. We slept in our sleeping bags in our two man tent. Roberto, our Mexican guide, slept in a tattered sleeping bag in the open. Marcos, our Tarahumara acquaintance, simply stretched out on the sand and went to sleep.

In 1963 a group of fifteen Americans attempted

to raft the Rio Urique through the Barranca del Cobre. Led by experienced river runners, the group had scouted the river from the air. What appeared from above to be long stretches of open channel turned out to be the river rushing down steep inclines, plunging over cliffs, and squirming through rock piles. The river proved to be extremely difficult for boating. Thirty foot high boulders are not uncommon in the Rio Urique and, at one point, the rafters began deflating their 400 pound rafts and rolling them like logs over the huge rocks. On some days the river running expedition progressed only a quarter of a mile. The ruggedness of the area is dramatized by the fact that these experienced river runners were forced to quit before they starved and hike up to the rim. As Michael Jenkinson has written, "In high water, the Urique may be the most violent river in America."

The group was helped out of the canyon by some Tarahumara who found them. O'Reilly, (in Sports Illustrated, 1963) a member of this expedition, writes, "Each one of us carried a canteen but nothing else. For five miles we climbed that trail, which seemed designed only for goats. At one point as we toiled upward the Indians passed us, each carrying a sixty pound pack of gear. Suddenly I realized that it was their third trip of the day."

The plight of the stalled expedition was reported and resulted in three days of newspaper, radio, and television stories about the lost party in the wilds of the Barranca del Cobre. Mexican planes flew over the area searching for the group, United States Army helicopters were dispatched, and paratroopers were almost used to jump into the canyon. Television commentator Chet Huntley described the canyon as one of the "most awesome chasms in the world" and so it is.

John Cross, the leader of the 1963 expedition, returned later that year and made it to below Divisadero in an inflatable kayak. He returned again in 1971 and filmed a documentary on the Rio Urique.

Not only is the terrain extremely rugged in the Barranca del Cobre, but the soil is quite poor. Yet the Tarahumara rely on the soil for almost their entire food supply. Animal manure is used extensively as fertilizer. Their main crop is corn, although beans, squash and chili are also important. The Tarahumara recognize six different kinds of corn, but an American botanist (Bye) has identified thirty-one types. Also, he has pinpointed thirteen types of beans and four kinds of chili. Together, these provide a nutritionally sound diet for the Tarahumara. Those who live deep in the canyons during the winter grow two crops of corn a year.

Given the primitive nature of their farming techniques (the most frequent method of plowing is with oxen pulling wooden plows), it is surprising to learn that the Tarahumara are constantly experimenting with crossbreeding new varieties of corn. Also the Tarahumara make extensive use of wild plants, collecting and eating some 120 varieties. Many of the wild plants we would consider to be weeds. In studying the Tarahumara, Bye observed that they have unconsciously begun the process of domesticating some of these.

In addition to their use as food, wild plants are utilized for many other purposes. The glue used in making violins comes from a lily bulb. Tobacco is raised and smoked. There are nineteen narcotic plants known to the Tarahumara. These are either feared and avoided or respected and used. The harvesting of medicinal wild plants is almost a business for a few Tarahumara, who carry their plants to Chihuahua or Juarez to be sold in markets. The

Tarahumara use nearly 300 different plants for medicinal purposes. Over the centuries the Tarahumara have learned to utilize the many assets of the Barranca del Cobre.

The Tarahumara walk or run up and down the canyons with relative ease, but for the average traveler hiking is difficult. As we have said many times, the canyon country is extremely rugged. The descent into the canyon is so precipitous that at one time it was the custom for non-Tarahumaras to deposit a stone at the foot of a large cross near the canyon rim while saying a prayer for safekeeping. This was done before the dangerous descent into the mighty barranca. Unless one is in excellent physical shape, we advise taking two days to descend to the Rio Urique. As in all steep mountain hiking, the trip down is harder on the feet and muscles than is the climb up.

Hiring a guide is advisable, and the rental of a burro to carry backpacks is a good idea. Both are very inexpensive. We arranged for our guide, Roberto Valenzuela, and his burro grande (large donkey), Porco, through the manager of a nearby lodge.

The Barranca del Cobre is one of those fantastic wonders of nature which must be seen to be believed. Rugged terrain, beautiful views, and a wild river at its bottom combine to make this one of the most outstanding canyons in North America, if not in the world. Even without considering that it is inhabited by the fantastic Tarahumara Indians, it is an incredible place.

PART IV

GETTING THERE

"Something hidden. Go and find it. Go and look
behind the ranges - Something lost behind the
ranges. Lost and waiting for you. Go."

Rudyard Kipling
"The Explorer"

Many Americans have longed to travel to interesting places and to visit interesting people. However, most do a lot more longing than traveling. Armchair adventuring is much easier than real adventuring. Limited finances, short vacations, and a "Can we really do it?" attitude keep people near home. They may do camping or backpacking, and see lovely places and have interesting experiences. But very few go on a safari to Africa, get acquainted with the tribes of New Guinea, or hike through a rugged country inhabited by primitive people living in caves.

The Barranca del Cobre and its inhabitants can be visited without a major investment of either time or money. A trip there is, at the same time, both manageable and adventuresome. One reason for the relative neglect of the Tarahumara by the traveler is the apprehension of so many Americans concerning travel in Mexico. In many ways Mexico is stranger to Americans than the countries of western Europe. The possibly contaminated water, the unclean food, the strange laws and language, and the occasional tales of police abuse do cause anxiety. Yet sickness, accidents, and unfortunate happenings occur everywhere from time to time and are not necessarily related to place. Halozone tablets for suspicious water, a careful selection of foods, as much knowledge of Spanish as possible, and a willingness to pace oneself and not get frustrated with others who do the same are all prerequisites to an enjoyable trip to Mexico. A satisfying visit to Mexico requires an attitude of flexibility and a willingness to learn, rather than to pass judgment.

One of the most astounding facts about the Tarahumara Indians is that they are located so close to the United States. A few years ago it was quite difficult to get to their region, but this is no longer true.

The railroad, particularly, is a very practical means of access to the beautiful Sierra Madre Occidental and to its amazing people, the Tarahumara. The Ferrocarriles Chihuahua al Pacifico line is part of the Mexican national railway system and runs for 569 miles (938 kilometers) from Ojinaga to Los Mochis near the Gulf of California. Ojinaga, Mexico is across the Rio Grande from Presidio, Texas. The railroad was completed in 1961 after nearly a century of development, financial schemes, and actual construction. During this time, interrupted by several wars and revolutions, the railroad companies were known by at least twelve different names. One of the building contractors on one stretch of the railroad was Pancho Villa. The rail line is one of the construction marvels of the world. The terrain it crosses is some of the roughest ever to be spanned by a railroad. In one area, the track makes a complete loop and passes under itself. This occurs in only three places in North America. There are many tunnels and bridges on the fantastic route. For an excellent account of this remarkable railroad see Joseph Wampler's 1969 book, NEW RAILS TO OLD TOWNS: THE REGION AND STORY OF THE FERROCARRILES CHIHUAHUA AL PACIFICO.

Travel on this line is surprisingly comfortable, especially if one takes the autovia (self-propelled car). The autovia is not only less crowded than the other types of cars, but it also has large windows which are a definite asset in enjoying the striking views. Food is available. The train ride is relatively informal and not without danger. Going downhill once from Divisadero to Creel, we were on the first of two autovias that were traveling together. The train stopped for over two hours along the way while the train crew scampered around with some very rusty tools. We were unable to tell what was going on, but they switched the rear car to the front and then started again. We guessed that probably the brakes had gone out on our car. Some months later, there was a serious accident near this spot.

Since the train schedule is not the same every day of the week, it is advisable to make inquiries locally. In Chihuahua, the train station for the Ferrocarriles Chihuahua al Pacifico is not the only station. It is possible to ship an auto by flatcar on this railroad, but we have not tried it and so will not recommend it.

Although the railroad is the preferred means of transportation into the Tarahumara country, it is not the only means. There are roads into the country from the east, but they are of uneven quality. Although we made the trip in a VW bug, a four wheel drive vehicle would make more sense.

A number of airstrips are also scattered throughout the Sierra Madre Occidental. Small planes can land on them, but there are no scheduled flights. The strip outside Creel is overlooked by caves which, at certain times of the year, are inhabited by Tarahumara families. This juxtaposition of the Stone Age and the Air Age we found to be fascinating.

Our first trip into Tarahumara country was by car. We drove from our home in Pueblo, Colorado to Creel. We knew of the existence of the railroad but wanted to drive to Creel if we could. We were not sure that it was possible. Having written to the Sanborn's office in El Paso, Texas in the late spring, we had been advised not to attempt the trip in the summer because of the danger from flash floods. Sanborn's specializes in selling car insurance to Americans driving into Mexico, but it also puts out directories and other information that is very helpful. It has offices in most of the American cities which are on the border with Mexico. If one is driving into Mexico or taking the train or bus, it would be worth the effort to stop in, or write, to Sanborn's.

We drove to Mexico in February. Driving from Colorado to Juarez, Mexico took one day. After spending the night at a hotel in Juarez, we drove to Chihuahua. In Chihuahua we stayed at the reasonably priced, yet lovely, Hotel Victoria. The next morning we drove west through Cuahtemoc and past La Junta. Some nine miles after the turnoff to La Junta and about ninety-six miles from Chihuahua we stopped for directions at a small police station near the top of a hill. The police (who were armed with rifles) pointed out for us the road to Creel. It was a faint track across a field. We had driven 881 miles from our home in Colorado and, at this point, left a paved road for the first time. We drove another fifty-four miles to Creel, but it took us four and one-half hours to make the trip!

The road was incredibly bad. There were fifteen streams to be forded (none had bridges). We drove over unbelievably rocky stretches and segments where there was no road visible. Our VW never got into third gear and was in first a good part of the time. Also, we frequently got lost, stopped to ask directions, and then backtracked. People along the way were generally not outgoing, but they were friendly and helpful.

The drive into the Sierra Madre was an emotional as well as a physical strain. For hours, we were unsure as to whether or not we were on the correct route. Passing through a strange country whose inhabitants spoke a different language and who were of uncertain friendliness (this was our first trip) was an unsettling experience. The frequent necessity of fording streams added to our anxiety, as did the lateness of the afternoon. Where the road was not rocky, it was frequently very muddy. Trucks had apparently been the only vehicles over this route and their high clearance and wide wheelbase made it impossible for our VW bug to follow their tracks through the mud. Every time we went through a mud hole, we felt a real fear of being high-centered and stranded. Once the strain became so great that we seriously considered turning back. This happened at a time when we were climbing through a pasture-like area along a faint trail. We decided to go to the top of the hill we were ascending before turning around. When we got to the top, we found another rise ahead which we decided to examine before giving up and returning. Mountain climbers know that there is always (it seems) another hill starting from the top of every hill one climbs. Soon the idea of turning around was forgotten.

At last we came into the little town of San Juanito. It had been a hard five hours from the end of the paved road near La Junta, only some thirty miles away. As we came into San Juanito late in the afternoon, we sought directions, knowing it was another twenty miles to Creel. Stopping a truck driver, we learned the way and then, just to check ourselves, asked him how far it was to Creel. In the usual Mexican fashion he answered in time rather than distance. His answer astounded us, and we guessed that we had misunderstood his Spanish. What we thought we heard him say was that it was only thirty minutes to Creel! We estimated that it would be closer to two hours and thirty minutes, but we traveled on. Soon, to our amazement, the rutty dirt road turned into a wide paved highway that led us to Creel in about thirty minutes. Our guess for the reason for this stretch of modern highway in the middle of a primitive mountain area is the fact that there is a sawmill in San Juanito and considerable logging around Creel. Undoubtedly, this road was built for log trucks.

Creel reminded us of a frontier town of, perhaps, the 1880s. The dusty unpaved streets, a bustling atmosphere, crude construction going on at a frantic pace, log buildings here and there, and the smell of freshly cut lumber all evoke the frontier town of the American West. We were astonished, therefore, to see children on their way to school carrying portable typewriters!

We stayed in Creel overnight and the next day took the train an hour and fifteen minutes to the breathtaking overlook at Divisadero.

The return drive from Creel to La Junta was better. Although lost several times, we generally found better roads and made it down in only three and one-half hours.

There are other ways of visiting this area that should be mentioned. Joseph Wampler leads tours through the Barranca del Cobre as well as other primitive areas of North America. His tours are primarily by train and minibus and generally do not involve backpacking. For more information write Wampler Tours, Box 45, Berkeley, California - 94701. Less expensive but more rustic tours are led periodically by the people who operate Colorado Adventuring, P. O. Box 293, Westcliffe, Colorado - 81252. Their trips involve backpacking to the Rio Urique. If one wants to rough it, but is not ready to go it alone, this outfit would be a good choice. Another company that advertises guided backpacking trips into the Barranca del Cobre is Outback Expeditions, P. O. Box 44, Terlingua, Texas - 79852. Others we have heard of are Sobek, Angels Camp, CA - 95222. They can be reached by telephone at (209) 736-4524. Also Rick Fisher, Sunracer Publications, P.O. Box 40092, Tucson, AZ - 85717. Telephone is (602) 881-0243.

After all of the comments on the ruggedness

of the country, it is pleasant to relate that there are several quite comfortable lodging places in the heart of the Tarahumara land. Two of these are in Creel and two in the Divisadero region.

In Creel the more comfortable place is the Parador el Montana. It is a modern motel located on the main street of Creel. One of our fondest memories is of the day we returned there after a hot, dusty exploration of the countryside to be surprised by the manager delivering two Margaritas to our room. They were "courtesy of the house" and very welcome. The Parador has a good restaurant and is about equal in price and comfort to a Ramada Inn. It appears to have a primarily Mexican clientele.

The other place we have stayed in Creel is the Hotel Nuevo. It is near the train station, economical, and yet clean. Our room had a fireplace (the only source of heat) and was quite comfortable. The manager warned us against drinking the tap water and pointed out a pitcher of water for drinking. We dropped in a halozone tablet just to be safe. The Hotel Nuevo has a dining room which is considerably less expensive than that of the Parador. The food is fair, but the most memorable feature of it is its relaxed atmosphere. While we were having dinner, a child led a goat through the dining room. Many Americans seem to be afraid of Mexico and of getting things stolen. One experience we had at the Hotel Nuevo in Creel was surprising and reassuring. After the hard drive, we had had dinner and fallen in a deep sleep in a comfortable bed in front of a fire in the fireplace. We were suddenly awakened by a pounding on the door and the manager's hysterical voice screaming. In our sleepiness it took us sometime to realize that the voice was repeating the Spanish words, "Su carro es abierto!" (Your car is open!) We stumbled out to our car with the manager and realized that she was simply telling us that our VW had been left unlocked. Nothing was missing. Evidently the manager had checked our car before going to bed, found it unlocked, and sounded the alarm! We had mixed feelings about being awakened, but neither then nor at any other time have we experienced any theft in Mexico.

There is at least one other place to stay in Creel. It is called Copper Canyon Lodge and is outside of town. The Copper Canyon Lodge has apparently developed much of its business from tours of Americans coming through Creel. It has a van that meets the trains and takes the tourists quickly out of Creel to this rather expensive-looking resort. We have never stayed there, but have the feeling that it is mainly for Americans who want to have little contact with the local people.

In Divisadero itself there is only one place to stay, the Hotel Divisadero. This is a canyon-rim lodge with one of the most beautiful views we have ever seen. The daily rate includes meals served family style in the main room. This room is comfortably furnished and drinks are available. The view out the picture windows and over the canyon is breathtaking. One of the outstanding new-old contrasts we experienced was in this room when we were sitting in front of the fireplace, drinks in hand, on our first evening in Divisadero. We looked up and out the side of the room to see a glow on a cliff a few hundred yards away — the fire of a family living in a cave.

It was also outside the Hotel Divisadero the next morning that we watched what was certainly the most beautiful sunrise we have ever seen.

About a mile or two down the railroad track west of Divisadero is a lodge called the Posada Barranca. Although not on the canyon rim, it is on a stop of the railroad and is a pleasant combination of the rustic and the comfortable. There is an English-speaking manager who helps greatly in making arrangements for a guide and in answering questions about the area.

The Posada Barranca was headquarters for our hike down to the Rio Urique. We had traveled from the United States with everything in our backpacks. In order to keep down the weight of our load, we had not carried extra pants. After our return from three days walking and two nights camping, we wanted to get our clothes washed; the lodge did that for us. We forgot that electric driers have not yet come to the Sierra Madre Occidental. Meal time passed before our pants were ready, and we were unable to go to the dining room to eat. The Posada staff graciously brought the meal to our room.

Coming from the west, a Tarahumara-bound auto traveler can go to Tuscon, Arizona and then south through Hermosillo, Mexico to the town of Los Mochis. Los Mochis has good accommodations and is located at the western end of the Ferrocarriles Chihuahua al Pacifico line. From here it is a relatively short trip into Tarahumara country.

An itinerary we found interesting and practical was to drive to El Paso, leave our car in an indoor parking lot, and walk across the Rio Grande into Juarez, Mexico. Since we were hiking, we took only our backpacks and traveled without luggage. From the Juarez customs office we took a taxi to the railroad station. At the Juarez station we bought tickets for the train to Chihuahua.

The city of Chihuahua is modern and industrial and has close to one-quarter of a million people living in it. It is situated 230 miles south of El Paso, Texas. We have also ridden the bus between Juarez and Chihuahua and have found it very comfortable. After staying overnight at a Chihuahua hotel, we then caught the railroad west to Divisadero.

Divisadero is not really a town, but it is the best overlook for the magnificent Barranca del Cobre. Every passenger train stops for twenty minutes at Divisadero to allow the passengers to get off and enjoy the spectacular view. Also a number of vendors (mostly Tarahumara women) sell souvenirs and artifacts here.

Hiking in the Sierra Madre is different in many ways from hiking in the United States. The only people in an American wilderness area are fellow hikers. This is definitely not the case in the Sierra Madre. People are there not because they are visiting, but because it is their home. Both while driving up into the mountains and hiking down into the canyons, we saw many people and sensed that there were many more. Although shy, the people would be helpful in a crisis. We commented about the fact that we were less isolated and safer than we would have been driving on some paved, but deserted, roads in the American West.

The Sierra Madre is not dry and forbidding like Baja California. At the season when American mountains are cold and wet, the Sierra Madre is ideal for hiking.

If one is tired of the hordes of visitors at American wilderness areas, one should try hiking in the Sierra Madre of northern Mexico. Hiking permits and quota systems are irrelevant, because very few people go there.

Backpackers, by definition, do not use pack animals and they seldom use guides. In the Sierra Madre a hiker is foolish if he does not use both. Good maps and almost any kind of signs are nonexistent.

Guides and pack animals are inexpensive. One can either ride or walk, or switch from one method of transportation to the other. Making contact with a guide is not difficult. Any responsible-looking person in the area can help one find a guide.

It's also useful to have some things along to give to people one meets, particularly hard candy for the children. Cigarettes for the men and safety pins for the women will be appreciated.

If one travels by car or intends to hike, he should avoid the rainy season. The insects can be extremely annoying in the wet months, while flash floods from the heavy rains can wipe out a trail or a road, leaving one stranded — or worse.

The Tarahumara country, despite its reputation for being inaccessible, is really quite easy to travel into. This is particularly true for the somewhat adventurous traveler who does not require the luxury and convenience that is so common in the United States. Transportation and accommodations are surprisingly good. For the person who has found this book about the Tarahumara Indians and their country interesting, there is little excuse not to make a visit.

THE END

BIBLIOGRAPHY

Abbey, Edward. "A Tale of the Sierra Madre." Mountain Gazette, July, 1975, pp. 10-17.

A well-written article that is pessimistic about the future of the Tarahumara and their land.

Balke, Bruno and Snow, Clyde. "Anthropological and Physiological Observations on Tarahumara Endurance Runners." American Journal of Physical Anthropology, September, 1965, pp. 293-301.

One of the better scientific expeditions studying the Tarahumara area.

Bennett, Wendell C. and Zingg, Robert M. The Tarahumara: An Indian Tribe of Northern Mexico. Chicago: The University of Chicago Press, 1935.

A detailed anthropological study with a large amount of information on the social and cultural life of the Tarahumara. Revised edition published in 1978.

Boudreau, Eugene. Trails of the Sierra Madre. Santa Barbara: Capra Press and San Francisco: Scrimshaw Press, 1973.

Valuable tips for the potential hiker. Covers areas of the Sierra Madre that are outside of Tarahumara country.

Burgess, Don. Podrias Vivir Como un Tarahumara? (How Would You Like to Live Like a Tarahumara?). Translated from Spanish for us by Judy Lutz. Mexico City: published by Bob Schalkwijk and Don Burgess. No date.

Question and answer book with pictures. Apparently designed for high school age youth. Written in Spanish.

Bye, Robert A. Jr. "Ethnoecology of the Tarahumara of Chihuahua, Mexico." Unpublished Ph. D. dissertation, Department of Biology, Harvard University, 1976.

Scientific summary, based on field studies and research, of all plants used by the Tarahumara. Emphasizes relationship between the plants and the Indians.

Cassel, Jonathan F. Tarahumara Indians. San Antonio: The Naylor Company, 1969.

An account of a family's hike to the Rio Urique, including their befriending of some Tarahumara.

Champion, J. R. "Acculturation Among the Tarahumara of Northwest Mexico Since 1890." Transactions of the New York Academy of Sciences, May, 1955, pp. 560-66.

Excellent anthropological study.

Clegg, Reed S., MD. "Tarahumara Indians." Rocky Mountain Medical Journal, January, 1972, pp. 57-58.

Short, but detailed on the physiological characteristics of the endurance runners.

Culin, Stewart. Games of the North American Indians. New York: Dover Publications, 1975.

A classic compendium originally published by the Government Printing Office in 1907 in the Twenty-Fourth Annual Report of the Bureau of American Ethnology to the

Smithsonian Institution, 1902-03, by W. H. Holmes, Chief.

Eigeland, Tor. "Canyons of the Tarahumara." In America's Majestic Canyons. National Geographic Society, 1979.

Beautiful pictures and a well-written article.

Elrick, Harold, et al. "Indians Who Run 100 Miles on 1500 Calories a Day." The Physician and Sportsmedicine, February, 1976, pp. 38-42.

Another scientific report on the Tarahumara. Not the best one.

Fayhee, M. John. "Bottoming Out in Mexico." Backpacker, November, 1987, pp. 48-53.

A first hand account of backpacking in the Barranca del Cobre. It is also the only article that stresses the tremendous beer drinking capacity of the Tarahumara.

Fixx, James F. The Complete Book of Running. New York: Random House, 1977.

The best book on running.

Fontana, Bernard L. Tarahumara: Where Night Is the Day of the Moon. Flagstaff, Arizona: Northland Press, 1979.

A beautiful volume, particularly strong on history, architecture, and the dances of the Tarahumara.

Fried, Jacob. "The Tarahumara." In Handbook of Middle American Indians, Edited by Evon Z. Vogt. Austin, Texas: University of Texas Press, 1969.

Describes many of the details of the culture. Includes several maps showing changes in the extent of the Tarahumara range since the 17th century.

Gadjusek, D. Carleton. "The Sierra Tarahumara." The Geographical Review, January, 1953, pp. 15-38.

One of the most complete and well-written articles in the literature.

Groom, Dale. "Cardiovascular Observations on the Tarahumara Indian Runners - the Modern Spartans." American Heart Journal, March, 1971, pp. 304-14.

Probably the most thorough of the physiological studies.

Jenkinson, Michael. "The Glory of the Long-Distance Runner." Natural History, January, 1972, pp. 54-65.

Well-written and interesting.

———. Wild Rivers of North America. New York: E. P. Dutton. 1973.

Includes material from the above article, but also contains a detailed description of rafting on the Rio Unique.

Kennedy, John G. "Tesguino Complex: The Role of Beer in Tarahumara Culture." American Anthropologist, June, 1963, pp. 620-40.

Good discussion of this important aspect of Tarahumara life.

———. Tarahumara of the Sierra Madre: Beer, ecology and social organization. Arlington Heights, Illinois: AHM

Publishing Corporation, 1978.

Excellent scholarly study of the Tarahumara culture. Repeats much of the earlier article.

Linton, Ralph, ed. <u>Acculturation in Seven American Indian Tribes</u>. New York: D. Appleton-Century Company, 1940.

Does not discuss the Tarahumara, but an invaluable aid in understanding them.

Lionnet, Andres. <u>Los Elementos de la Lengua Tarahumara</u>. Mexico City, Mexico: Instituto de Investigaciones Historico, Universidad Nacional Autonoma de Mexico, 1972.

A discussion of the Tarahumara language. Written in Spanish.

Lumholtz, Carl. <u>Unknown Mexico</u>. New York: Charles Scribner's, 1902.

Classic, detailed 2 volume scientific analysis of several Mexican Indian tribes, including the Tarahumara.

Merrill, William L. "God's Saviours in the Sierra Madre." <u>Natural History</u>, March, 1983, pp. 59-66.

The best account of the religious rituals and beliefs of the Tarahumara.

Moore, Robert Thomas. "The Descent to the Barranca del Cobre." <u>Natural History</u>, January, 1951, pp. 34 ff.

Brief account of a backpacking journey in the days before the railroad.

Norman, James. "The Tarahumaras: Mexico's Long Distance Runners." National Geographic, May 1976, pp. 702-18.

Good summary of the Tarahumara. Excellent pictures.

O'Reilly, Mary Ellen. "Lady on a River of Rock." Sports Illustrated, October 21, 1963, pp. 26-33.

Account of the river-running expedition mentioned in the text.

Pennington, Campbell W. The Tarahumar of Mexico. Salt Lake City: University of Utah Press, 1963.

Scientific study based on field work and scholarly research. Excellent.

Pritikin, Nathan. The Pritikin Program for Diet and Exercise. New York: Grosset and Dunlap, 1979.

A bestseller.

Seegers, Scott and Seegers, Kathleen. "The Most Dramatic Train Ride in the Hemisphere." Reader's Digest, May, 1974, pp. 184 ff.

About the Ferrocarrile Chihuahua al Pacifico.

Shrake, Edwin. "A Lonely Tribe of Long-Distance Runners." Sports Illustrated, January, 1967, pp. 56-62, 65-67.

Another account of a short expedition.

Stratton, R., Blackburn, M., Andress, D., and Zeiner, A. "Exercise Stress-Induced Heart Rate and Blood Pressure Changes Among Male Tarahumara Indians and World Class

Athletes." <u>Psychophysiology</u>, March, 1981, P. 165.

The only comparative physiological study.

Tisdale, Frederick. "The Greatest Long-Distance Runners in the World." <u>The Mentor</u>, March, 1928, pp. 19-20.

One of the earliest accounts.

Wampler, Joseph. <u>New Rails to Old Towns: The Region and Story of the Ferrocarriles Chihuahua al Pacifico</u>. Berkeley, California: self-published, 1969.

The only book that focuses on the railroad.

Zingg, Robert M. "Christmasing with the Tarahumaras." In <u>Coyote Wisdom</u>, Edited by J. Frank Dobie, et al. Austin, Texas: Texas Folklore Society Publications, 1938, pp. 207-24.

Fascinating account of a holiday celebration with the Tarahumara.

———. "The Genuine and Spurious Values in Tarahumara Culture." <u>American Anthropologist</u>, January-March, 1942, pp. 78-92.

Somewhat hard to understand, but interesting.

INDEX

DIMI PRESS PRODUCTS FOR YOU

TAPES are available for........................$9.95 each

16 different titles:
#1-LIVE LONGER, RELAX
#2-ACTIVE RELAXATION
#3-CONQUER YOUR SHYNESS
#4-CONQUER YOUR DEPRESSION
#5-CONQUER YOUR FEARS
#6-CONQUER YOUR INSOMNIA
#7-CONTROL YOUR CANCER
#8-LAST LONGER, ENJOY SEX MORE
#9-WEIGHT CONTROL
#10-STOP SMOKING
#11-LIVE LONGER, RELAX(female voice)
#12-ACTIVE RELAXATION(female voice)
#13-UNWIND WHILE DRIVING
#14-RELAX AWHILE
#15-RELAX ON THE BEACH/MEADOW
#16-HOW TO MEDITATE

TAPE ALBUM has six-cassettes and is called:

GUIDE TO RELAXATION.........$49.95

BOOKS:

THE RUNNING INDIANS is this book and
a copy can be bought for............$11.95

FEEL BETTER! LIVE LONGER! RELAX by
Richard L. Lutz is a manual of relaxation
techniques.................................$9.95

ORDER FORM

DIMI-TAPES #_____x9.95=_____

GUIDE TO RELAXATION___49.95=_____

FEEL BETTER! LIVE LONGER!
RELAX_____9.95=_____

THE RUNNING INDIANS___11.95=_____

Postage & handling_____2.00

TOTAL _____

_____Check or money order

_____VISA/MC Account #_____

Exp. Date_____Signature_____

Name_____

Address_____

City/State/Zip_____

Phone(_____)_____

Mail to: **DIMI PRESS**
                  P.O. Box 3363
                  Salem, OR   97302
Phone: **(503) 364-7698**